Low Fat

GREAT-TASTING™

HOT & SPICY

Healthy & Delicious Recipes

PUBLICATIONS INTERNATIONAL, LTD.

Food Guide Pyramid source: U.S. Department of Agriculture/U.S. Department of Health and Human Services.

Recipe Development: Nanette Blanchard, Sandra Day, Carla Muscat
Nutritional Analysis: Linda R. Yoakam, M.S., R.D.

Photography: Photo/Kevin Smith, Chicago
Photographers: Kevin Smith, Doug Hunter
Prop Stylists: Lucianne Crowley, Diane Gurolnick
Food Stylists: Tobe LeMoine, Teri Rys-Maki
Assistant Food Stylist: Laura Hess
Photo Assistants: Jerry Cox, Greg Shapps

Pictured on the front cover *(from left to right):* Jalapeño Cole Slaw *(page 84)* and Spicy Island Chicken *(page 22).*
Pictured on the inside front cover: Spicy Lentil and Chick-Pea Soup *(page 20).*
Pictured on the inside back cover: South-of-the-Border Pizza *(page 68).*
Pictured on the back cover *(clockwise from top left):* Confetti Black Beans *(page 90),* Couscous with Chick-Peas and Vegetables *(page 70),* Cajun-Style Corn with Crayfish *(page 62)* and Grilled Flank Steak with Horseradish Sauce *(page 52).*

CONTENTS

LESSONS IN SMART EATING

Today, people everywhere are more aware than ever before of the importance of maintaining a healthful lifestyle. In addition to proper exercise, this includes eating foods that are lower in fat, sodium and cholesterol. The goal of this book is to provide today's cook with easy-to-prepare recipes that taste great, yet easily fit into your dietary goals. Eating well is a matter of making smarter choices about the foods you eat. Preparing these recipes is your first step toward making smart choices a delicious reality.

A Balanced Diet

The U.S. Department of Agriculture and the Department of Health and Human Services have developed a Food Guide Pyramid to illustrate how easy it is to eat a healthier diet. It is not a rigid prescription, but rather a general guide that lets you choose a healthful diet that's right for you. It calls for eating a wide variety of foods to get the nutrients you need and, at the same time, the right amount of calories to maintain a healthy weight.

Food Guide Pyramid
A Guide to Daily Food Choices

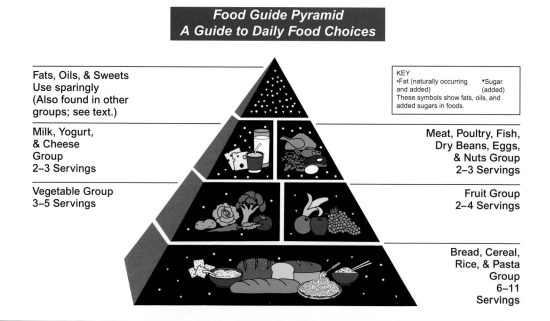

Fats, Oils, & Sweets
Use sparingly
(Also found in other
groups; see text.)

KEY
•Fat (naturally occurring   ▾Sugar
and added)   (added)
These symbols show fats, oils, and
added sugars in foods.

Milk, Yogurt,
& Cheese
Group
2–3 Servings

Meat, Poultry, Fish,
Dry Beans, Eggs,
& Nuts Group
2–3 Servings

Vegetable Group
3–5 Servings

Fruit Group
2–4 Servings

Bread, Cereal,
Rice, & Pasta
Group
6–11
Servings

The number of servings, and consequently, the number of calories a person can eat each day, is determined by a number of factors, including age, weight, height, activity level and gender. Sedentary women and some older adults need about 1,600 calories each day. For most children, teenage girls, active women and many sedentary men 2,000 calories is about right. Teenage boys, active men and some very active women use about 2,800 calories each day. Use the chart below to determine how many servings you need for your calorie level.

Personalized Food Group Servings for Different Calorie Levels*			
	1,600	2,000	2,800
Bread Group Servings	6	8	11
Vegetable Group Servings	3	4	5
Fruit Group Servings	2	3	4
Milk Group Servings	2–3**	2–3**	2–3**
Meat Group Servings (ounces)	5	6	7

* Numbers may be rounded.
** Women who are pregnant or breast-feeding, teenagers and young adults to age 24 need 3 or more servings.

Lower Fat for Healthier Living

It is widely known that most Americans' diets are too high in fat. A low fat diet reduces your risk of getting certain diseases and helps you maintain a healthy weight. Studies have shown that eating more than the recommended amount of fat (especially saturated fat) is associated with increased blood cholesterol levels in some adults. A high blood cholesterol level is associated with increased risk for heart disease. A high fat diet may also increase your chances for obesity and some types of cancer.

Nutrition experts recommend diets that contain 30% or less of total daily calories from fat. The "30% calories from fat" goal applies to a total diet over time, not to a single food, serving of a recipe or meal. To find the approximate percentage of calories from fat use this easy 3-step process:

1 Multiply the grams of fat per serving by 9 (there are 9 calories in each gram of fat) to give you the number of calories from fat per serving.

2 Divide by the total number of calories per serving.

3 Multiply by 100%.

For example, imagine a 200 calorie sandwich that has 10 grams of fat.
To find the percentage of calories from fat, first multiply the grams of fat by 9:
$$10 \times 9 = 90$$

Then, divide by the total number of calories in a serving:
$$90 \div 200 = .45$$

Multiply by 100% to get the percentage of calories from fat:
$$.45 \times 100\% = 45\%$$

You may find doing all this math tiresome, so an easier way to keep track of the fat in your diet is to calculate the total *grams* of fat appropriate to your caloric intake, then keep a running count of fat grams over the course of a day. The Nutrition Reference Chart on page 92 lists recommended daily fat intakes based on calorie level.

Defining "Fat Free"

It is important to take the time to read food labels carefully. For example, you'll find many food products on the grocery store shelves making claims such as "97% fat free." This does not necessarily mean that 97% of the *calories* are free from fat (or that only 3% of calories come from fat). Often these numbers are calculated by weight. This means that out of 100 grams of this food, 3 grams are fat. Depending on what else is in the food, the percentage of calories from fat can be quite high. You may find that the percent of calories *from fat* can be as high as 50%.

Daily Values

Fat has become the focus of many diets and eating plans. This is because most Americans' diets are too high in fat. However, there are other important nutrients to be aware of, including saturated fat, sodium, cholesterol, protein, carbohydrates and several vitamins and minerals. Daily values for these nutrients have been established by the government and reflect current nutritional recommendations for a 2,000 calorie reference diet. They are appropriate for most adults and children (age 4 or older) and provide excellent guidelines for an overall healthy diet. The chart on page 92 gives the daily values for 11 different items.

Nutritional Analysis

Every recipe is accompanied by a nutritional analysis block that lists certain nutrient values for a single serving.

■ The analysis of each recipe includes all the ingredients that are listed in that recipe, *except* ingredients labeled as "optional" or "for garnish."

■ If a range is given in the yield of a recipe ("Makes 6 to 8 servings" for example), the *lower* yield was used to calculate the per serving information.

■ If a range is offered for an ingredient ("¼ to ⅛ teaspoon" for example), the *first* amount given was used to calculate the nutritional information.

■ If an ingredient is presented with an option ("2 cups hot cooked rice or noodles" for example), the *first* item listed was used to calculate the nutritional information.

■ Foods shown in photographs on the same serving plate and offered as "serve with" suggestions at the end of a recipe are *not* included in the recipe analysis unless they are listed in the ingredient list.

■ Meat should be trimmed of all visible fat since this is reflected in the nutritional analysis.

■ In recipes calling for cooked rice or noodles, the analysis was based on rice or noodles that were prepared without added salt or fat unless otherwise mentioned in the recipe.

The nutrition information that appears with each recipe was calculated by an independent nutrition consulting firm. Every effort has been made to check the accuracy of these numbers. However, because numerous variables account for a wide range of values in certain foods, all analyses that appear in this book should be considered approximate.

The recipes in this publication are *not* intended as a medically therapeutic program, nor as a substitute for medically approved diet plans for people on fat, cholesterol or sodium restricted diets. You should consult your physician before beginning any diet plan. The recipes offered here can be a part of a healthy lifestyle that meets recognized dietary guidelines. A healthy lifestyle includes not only eating a balanced diet, but engaging in proper exercise as well.

All the ingredients called for in these recipes are generally available in large supermarkets, so there is no need to go to specialty or health food stores. You'll also see an ever-increasing amount of reduced fat and nonfat products available in local markets. Take advantage of these items to reduce your daily fat intake even more.

Cooking Healthier

When cooking great-tasting low fat meals, you will find some techniques or ingredients are different from traditional cooking. Fat serves as a flavor enhancer and gives foods a distinctive and desirable texture. In order to compensate for the lack of fat and still give great-tasting results, many of these recipes call for a selection of herbs or a combination of fresh vegetables. A wide variety of grains and pastas are also used. Many of the recipes call for alternative protein sources, such as dried beans or tofu. Often meat is included in a recipe as an accent flavor rather than the star attraction. Vegetables are often "sautéed" in a small amount of broth rather than oil. Applesauce may be added to baked goods to give a texture similar to full fat foods. These are all simple changes that you can easily make when you start cooking healthy!

Cooking Hot & Spicy

Preparing hot and spicy recipes that are both healthy *and* delicious is actually very simple. Cooking with chilies and lots of herbs and spices results in bold, exciting flavors—so it's easy to reduce the amount of salt and fat in recipes. Many spicy dishes are full of fresh vegetables and high-fiber grains to further enhance their nutritional value. Supermarkets today offer a tremendous variety of fresh produce, pastas, grains and beans that can spice up your meals with interesting flavors and textures while providing excellent health benefits at the same time. This sensational collection of recipes will convince you that good nutrition and good taste can be a very successful and savory combination.

Both heat and spice in recipes are produced by a wide variety of food sources. Chili peppers, the most common and well-known sources of heat, are used in dishes worldwide from Mexico to Africa to Asia and beyond. Cooking with chilies is a matter of individual taste—what seems incredibly hot to one person may taste mild or dull to another. Those people who enjoy very hot food can always add more chilies than a recipe suggests or use a hotter variety of chili pepper. (For example, serrano peppers may be substituted for jalapeños for more heat.) Many supermarkets have large produce sections that carry a number of different chilies; ask for assistance if you are not certain which are the hotter ones.

Another method of adjusting the heat in recipes depends on the way the chilies are prepared . Much of a chili pepper's heat is in the seeds, veins (the thin inner membranes to which the seeds are attached) and the parts nearest to the veins, so removing these parts before cooking will greatly reduce the hotness of the dish. Whether you retain the seeds and veins for maximum heat or remove and discard them, you should exercise caution when handling chilies. Wear rubber gloves if you have especially sensitive skin or if you will be handling a number of chilies, as the oil from the seeds and veins can sting and irritate the skin. Avoid touching your eyes, and always wash your hands thoroughly when finished.

In addition to fresh chili peppers, you'll find that fiery hot flavors come from many chili pepper by-products, such as hot pepper sauce, ground red pepper, red pepper flakes, chili sauce and chili paste. The same guidelines of personal taste apply with these ingredients: use as much or as little as suits your personal taste. Also, remember that the heat from cooking will slightly intensify the hot pepper flavors, so allow some time for these flavors to develop before adding more of whichever pepper product you are using.

For a different kind of heat, recipes may call for a healthy dose of peppercorns, a dab or two of hot mustard, a dash of curry, a dollop of horseradish or a splash of vinegar. Fresh ginger also provides heat and spice, although it is generally considered too hot and pungent to eat raw. The strong heat and flavor of ginger mellows with cooking, as is the case with mustard, horseradish and garlic.

Big, bold flavors can also come from more familiar sources, such as fresh or dried herbs and spices. Adding new zip and zing to an old favorite might be as simple as increasing the amount of herbs in the recipe. Or, try a more complex or unusual blend of herbs for a zesty change of pace. Salsas, barbecue sauces and spice rubs are all examples of this technique, which combines intense, vibrant flavors to create healthy, mouthwatering dishes. You'll find that cooking healthy can be more flavorful than you ever imagined. So go ahead—turn up the heat and spice up your life!

APPETIZERS

BLACK BEAN SALSA

1 can (14½ ounces) black beans, rinsed and drained
1 cup frozen whole kernel corn, thawed
1 large tomato, chopped
¼ cup chopped green onions
2 tablespoons chopped fresh cilantro
2 tablespoons lemon juice
1 tablespoon vegetable oil
1 teaspoon chili powder
¼ teaspoon salt
6 corn tortillas

1 Combine beans, corn, tomato, green onions, cilantro, lemon juice, oil, chili powder and salt in medium bowl; mix well.

2 Preheat oven to 400°F. Cut each tortilla into 8 wedges; place on ungreased baking sheet. Bake 6 to 8 minutes or until edges begin to brown. Serve tortilla wedges warm or at room temperature with salsa. Garnish with lemon wedges and additional fresh cilantro, if desired.

Makes 6 servings

❖

Black beans provide a dramatic background for a burst of brilliant colors and bright flavors. Enjoy this salsa over grilled fish or chicken, or simply with a basket of warm tortillas.

❖

Nutrients per Serving:

Calories	161
(18% of calories from fat)	
Total Fat	4 g
Saturated Fat	<1 g
Cholesterol	0 mg
Sodium	351 mg
Carbohydrate	31 g
Dietary Fiber	5 g
Protein	8 g
Calcium	51 mg
Iron	1 mg
Vitamin A	55 RE
Vitamin C	9 mg

DIETARY EXCHANGES:
2 Starch/Bread, ½ Fat

ASIAN NOODLE SOUP

Just what the doctor ordered—this chicken soup explodes with the bright Asian flavors of ginger, garlic and cilantro. A dash of hot chili oil (available in the Oriental foods section of the supermarket) adds just the right amount of heat.

Nutrients per Serving:

Calories 118
(30% of calories from fat)
Total Fat 4 g
Saturated Fat <1 g
Cholesterol 4 mg
Sodium 152 mg
Carbohydrate 17 g
Dietary Fiber 3 g
Protein 4 g
Calcium 48 mg
Iron 1 mg
Vitamin A 33 RE
Vitamin C 19 mg

DIETARY EXCHANGES:
½ Starch/Bread,
1½ Vegetable, 1 Fat

---

4 ounces dried Chinese egg noodles
3 cans (14 ounces each) ⅓-less-salt chicken broth
2 slices fresh ginger
2 cloves garlic, peeled and cut into halves
½ cup fresh snow peas, cut into 1-inch pieces
3 tablespoons chopped green onions
1 tablespoon chopped fresh cilantro
1½ teaspoons hot chili oil
½ teaspoon Oriental sesame oil

1 Cook noodles according to package directions, omitting salt. Drain and set aside.

2 Combine chicken broth, ginger and garlic in large saucepan; bring to a boil over high heat. Reduce heat to low; simmer about 15 minutes. Remove ginger and garlic with slotted spoon and discard.

3 Add snow peas, green onions, cilantro, chili oil and sesame oil to broth; simmer 3 to 5 minutes. Stir in noodles; serve immediately. Garnish with red chili pepper strips, if desired.

Makes 4 servings

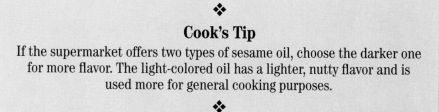

Cook's Tip
If the supermarket offers two types of sesame oil, choose the darker one for more flavor. The light-colored oil has a lighter, nutty flavor and is used more for general cooking purposes.

ROASTED EGGPLANT DIP

❖

Baba ghanoush is the name of this traditional and healthy Middle Eastern appetizer. For the best flavor, choose firm, smooth-skinned eggplants for roasting. You can reduce the fat content of the dip by pouring any oil off the top of the tahini before measuring it.

❖

2 eggplants (about 1 pound each)
3 tablespoons sesame tahini*
¼ cup lemon juice
4 cloves garlic, minced
2 teaspoons hot pepper sauce
½ teaspoon salt
  Paprika
1 tablespoon chopped fresh parsley

1 Prick eggplants in several places with fork. To roast over charcoal, place eggplants on grill over hot coals; cook about 30 to 40 minutes or until skin is black and blistered and pulp is soft, turning often. To roast in oven, preheat oven to 450°F. Place eggplants on baking sheet; bake about 30 to 40 minutes or until skin is blistered and pulp is soft.

2 Peel eggplants when cool enough to handle. Let cool to room temperature.

3 Place eggplant pulp in food processor with tahini, lemon juice, garlic, hot pepper sauce and salt; process until smooth. Refrigerate at least 1 hour before serving to allow flavors to blend. Sprinkle dip with paprika and parsley; serve with pita bread wedges. Garnish with red chili pepper slices, if desired. *Makes 8 (¼-cup) servings*

*Tahini is available in the ethnic section of the supermarket or in Middle Eastern grocery stores.

Nutrients per Serving:	
Calories	49
(26% of calories from fat)	
Total Fat	2 g
Saturated Fat	<1 g
Cholesterol	0 mg
Sodium	144 mg
Carbohydrate	9 g
Dietary Fiber	3 g
Protein	2 g
Calcium	18 mg
Iron	1 mg
Vitamin A	9 RE
Vitamin C	7 mg

DIETARY EXCHANGES:
½ Fat

❖

Cook's Tip

Eggplants become bitter with age, so do not purchase them too far in advance of cooking (1 to 2 days for best flavor).

❖

SAVORY CORN CAKES

Try a new hors d'oeuvre at your next party and listen to the raves! Smoked cheese provides an extra flavor boost that's impossible to resist. The supermarket cheese case should have several selections, or check in a specialty wine and cheese shop.

❖

2 cups all-purpose flour
1 teaspoon baking powder
½ teaspoon salt
2 cups frozen whole kernel corn, thawed
1 cup skim milk
1 cup (4 ounces) shredded smoked Cheddar cheese
2 egg whites, beaten
1 whole egg, beaten
4 green onions, finely chopped
2 cloves garlic, minced
1 tablespoon chili powder
    Prepared salsa (optional)

1 Combine flour, baking powder and salt in large bowl with wire whisk. Stir in corn, milk, cheese, egg whites, egg, green onions, garlic and chili powder until well blended.

2 Spray large nonstick skillet with nonstick cooking spray; heat over medium-high heat.

3 Drop batter by ¼ cupfuls into skillet. Cook 3 minutes per side or until golden brown. Serve with prepared salsa.   *Makes 12 cakes*

Nutrients per Serving:

1 cake

Calories	152
(19% of calories from fat)	
Total Fat	3 g
Saturated Fat	2 g
Cholesterol	25 mg
Sodium	227 mg
Carbohydrate	25 g
Dietary Fiber	1 g
Protein	6 g
Calcium	91 mg
Iron	1 mg
Vitamin A	72 RE
Vitamin C	2 mg

DIETARY EXCHANGES:
1½ Starch/Bread, ½ Fat

❖

Cook's Tip
Semi-firm cheeses like Cheddar are easier to grate when cold. They can also be grated ahead of time and stored in plastic bags in the refrigerator until ready to use.

❖

SPICY LENTIL AND CHICK-PEA SOUP

Inspired by a traditional Moroccan sauce called harissa, this flavorful soup is a great source of fiber and iron. Soaking dried beans overnight allows them to cook faster and rids them of gas-producing carbohydrates.

Nutrients per Serving:

Calories	188
(9% of calories from fat)	
Total Fat	2 g
Saturated Fat	<1 g
Cholesterol	0 mg
Sodium	241 mg
Carbohydrate	35 g
Dietary Fiber	3 g
Protein	10 g
Calcium	78 mg
Iron	4 mg
Vitamin A	90 RE
Vitamin C	42 mg

DIETARY EXCHANGES:
2 Starch/Bread,
1 Vegetable, ½ Fat

½ cup dried chick-peas (garbanzo beans)
4 cans (14 ounces each) ⅓-less-salt chicken broth
1 cup dried lentils
1 large onion, chopped
1 rib celery, chopped
1 teaspoon ground turmeric
½ teaspoon salt
½ teaspoon ground cinnamon
½ teaspoon black pepper
¼ teaspoon ground ginger
¼ teaspoon ground red pepper
¼ cup uncooked rice
3 cups chopped ripe tomatoes
¼ cup chopped fresh parsley
2 tablespoons chopped fresh cilantro
6 lemon wedges

1 Sort and rinse chick-peas; place in large saucepan. Cover with water and let soak overnight; drain chick-peas and return to saucepan. Add chicken broth to saucepan; bring to a boil over high heat. Reduce heat to low; cover and simmer 1 hour.

2 Sort and rinse lentils; add to chick-peas with onion, celery, turmeric, salt, cinnamon, black pepper, ginger and ground red pepper. Cover and simmer 45 minutes or until lentils are tender.

3 Stir in rice and tomatoes; bring to a boil over medium-high heat. Reduce heat to low; cover and simmer 20 to 25 minutes or until rice is tender.

4 Stir in parsley and cilantro; simmer 5 minutes. Serve with lemon wedges; garnish with additional fresh cilantro, if desired. *Makes 6 servings*

POULTRY

SPICY ISLAND CHICKEN

❖

Savor the flavor of the tropics in your own backyard! Try to marinate the chicken the night before so the spices have time to take full effect.

❖

Nutrients per Serving:

Calories	203
(30% of calories from fat)	
Total Fat	7 g
Saturated Fat	1 g
Cholesterol	73 mg
Sodium	421 mg
Carbohydrate	8 g
Dietary Fiber	1 g
Protein	28 g
Calcium	52 mg
Iron	2 mg
Vitamin A	40 RE
Vitamin C	10 mg

DIETARY EXCHANGES:
3 Lean Meat, ½ Vegetable, ½ Fat

1 cup finely chopped white onion
⅓ cup white wine vinegar
6 green onions, finely chopped
6 cloves garlic, minced
1 habañero or serrano pepper, finely chopped
4½ teaspoons fresh thyme leaves *or* 2 teaspoons dried thyme leaves, crushed
4½ teaspoons olive oil
1 tablespoon ground allspice
2 teaspoons sugar
1 teaspoon salt
1 teaspoon ground cinnamon
1 teaspoon ground nutmeg
1 teaspoon black pepper
½ teaspoon ground red pepper
6 boneless skinless chicken breast halves

1 Combine all ingredients except chicken in medium bowl; mix well. Place chicken in resealable plastic food storage bag and add seasoning mixture; turn bag to coat. Marinate in refrigerator 4 hours or overnight.

2 Spray cold grid with nonstick cooking spray. Adjust grid to 4 to 6 inches above heat. Preheat grill to medium-high heat.

3 Remove chicken from marinade. Grill 5 to 7 minutes per side or until chicken is no longer pink in center, brushing occasionally with marinade. Discard remaining marinade. Serve with grilled sweet potatoes. Garnish, if desired. *Makes 6 servings*

CURRIED CHICKEN CUTLETS

Dredging chicken in seasoned flour gives these cutlets a tasty, golden-brown coating. Bits of flour left in the skillet after cooking also help to thicken the piquant lemony sauce made right in the pan.

❖

Nutrients per Serving:

Calories	230
(18% of calories from fat)	
Total Fat	5 g
Saturated Fat	1 g
Cholesterol	73 mg
Sodium	599 mg
Carbohydrate	17 g
Dietary Fiber	1 g
Protein	29 g
Calcium	34 mg
Iron	2 mg
Vitamin A	273 RE
Vitamin C	97 mg

DIETARY EXCHANGES:
1 Starch/Bread, 3 Lean Meat

4 boneless skinless chicken breast halves
½ cup all-purpose flour
1 tablespoon curry powder
1 teaspoon salt
1 teaspoon ground red pepper
2 red bell peppers, cut lengthwise into ¼-inch-thick slices
1 teaspoon olive oil
¼ cup lemon juice
¼ cup finely chopped fresh cilantro

1 Pound chicken breasts to ¼-inch thickness between 2 pieces of plastic wrap with flat side of meat mallet or rolling pin.

2 Combine flour, curry powder, salt and ground red pepper in shallow bowl. Dip chicken cutlets in flour mixture to coat both sides well; shake off excess flour.

3 Generously spray nonstick skillet with nonstick cooking spray; heat over medium heat. Add 2 chicken cutlets; cook 3 to 4 minutes per side. Transfer to warm plate; cover and set aside. Repeat with remaining chicken.

4 Add bell peppers and olive oil to skillet; cook and stir 5 minutes or until peppers are tender. Stir in lemon juice and cilantro; heat through. Pour sauce over chicken cutlets. Garnish with kale and fresh marjoram, if desired. *Makes 4 servings*

❖

Cook's Tip
Curry powder is a spice that gets hotter the longer it stands, so use caution when adding it to a dish that will not be eaten right away.

❖

TURKEY CHILI

❖

*Don't just buy any ground
turkey, since much of it is
quite high in fat. First be
sure that the label says
"ground turkey breast" to get
the leanest meat possible.
Then cook up a big pot of
healthy, hearty chili to enjoy
over rice or with a warm
batch of Spicy Corn Muffins
(page 88).*

❖

Nutrients per Serving:

Calories	220
(12% of calories from fat)	
Total Fat	3 g
Saturated Fat	1 g
Cholesterol	33 mg
Sodium	745 mg
Carbohydrate	30 g
Dietary Fiber	3 g
Protein	23 g
Calcium	89 mg
Iron	3 mg
Vitamin A	200 RE
Vitamin C	68 mg

DIETARY EXCHANGES:
1 Starch/Bread, 2 Lean
Meat, 2 Vegetable

1 pound extra-lean ground turkey breast
1 cup chopped onion
1 cup chopped green bell pepper
3 cloves garlic, minced
3 cans (14½ ounces each) chopped tomatoes
½ cup water
1 tablespoon chili powder
1 teaspoon ground cinnamon
1 teaspoon ground cumin
½ teaspoon paprika
½ teaspoon dried oregano leaves, crushed
½ teaspoon black pepper
¼ teaspoon salt
1 can (16 ounces) pinto beans, rinsed and drained

1 Spray large skillet with nonstick cooking spray. Cook turkey, onion, bell pepper and garlic over medium-high heat about 5 minutes or until turkey begins to brown, stirring frequently and breaking up turkey with back of spoon.

2 Stir in tomatoes; cook 5 minutes. Add water, chili powder, cinnamon, cumin, paprika, oregano, black pepper and salt; mix well. Stir in beans.

3 Bring to a boil; reduce heat to medium-low. Simmer about 30 minutes or until chili thickens. Garnish, if desired. *Makes 4 servings*

❖

Health Note
Cooked pinto beans have an impressive 5.9 grams of fiber per ½-cup serving, which can help in lowering your level of LDL (bad) cholesterol.

❖

CHICKEN ETOUFFÉE

❖

Browning flour in a skillet is the secret behind creating a healthy version of this classic Cajun dish. Eliminating the usual roux—a blend of butter and flour—from the recipe removes much of the fat while still allowing the distinctive flavors of the dish to come through.

❖

Dry Roux (page 30)
4 chicken breast halves
¾ teaspoon salt
½ teaspoon ground red pepper
¼ teaspoon black pepper
1 tablespoon vegetable oil
3 cups chopped yellow onions
½ cup chopped green bell pepper
1 cup water, divided
3 large cloves garlic, minced
3 cups ⅓-less-salt chicken broth
¼ cup chopped green onions

1 Prepare Dry Roux.

2 Remove skin and fat from chicken. Combine salt, ground red pepper and black pepper in cup; sprinkle 1 teaspoon mixture over chicken. Heat oil in large heavy skillet over medium heat. Add chicken; cover and cook about 20 minutes or until browned on all sides, draining any liquid in pan halfway through cooking time.

3 Remove chicken from skillet. Add yellow onions and bell pepper; cover and cook 10 to 15 minutes or until onions begin to brown, stirring occasionally. Add ⅓ cup water and increase heat to medium-high. Cook about 10 minutes or until mixture begins to stick and brown again, stirring frequently and watching carefully to prevent burning. Add ⅓ cup water; cook and stir until mixture begins to stick and brown again. Add remaining ⅓ cup water and garlic; cook until mixture begins to stick and brown again, stirring frequently.

4 Stir in chicken broth; bring to a boil over medium-high heat. Quickly whisk in Dry Roux until smooth and well mixed; cook 5 minutes. Add chicken and remaining ½ teaspoon salt mixture to skillet; bring to a boil.

5 Reduce heat to medium-low; simmer about 15 minutes or until mixture is thickened and chicken is no longer pink in center. Sprinkle with green onions. Serve over rice. Garnish with green bell pepper and carrot, if desired.

Makes 4 servings

(continued on page 30)

Chicken Etouffée, continued

Nutrients per Serving:	
Calories	279
(24% of calories from fat)	
Total Fat	7 g
Saturated Fat	1 g
Cholesterol	73 mg
Sodium	497 mg
Carbohydrate	22 g
Dietary Fiber	3 g
Protein	31 g
Calcium	59 mg
Iron	2 mg
Vitamin A	58 RE
Vitamin C	36 mg

DIETARY EXCHANGES:
3 Lean Meat, 2 Vegetable,
½ Fat

DRY ROUX

⅓ cup all-purpose flour

1 Heat medium nonstick skillet over medium-high heat about 3 minutes. Add flour to skillet; cook 10 to 15 minutes or until flour turns the color of peanut butter or light cinnamon, stirring frequently to prevent burning. Sift flour into small bowl; set aside.

❖

Cook's Tips

Purchase poultry with a U.S.D.A. Grade A rating. Make sure the package is secure and unbroken and the sell-by date has not passed.

Poultry meat should not look gray or pasty and should not have any noticeable odor.

Packaged poultry should not have any accumulated liquid on the tray or in the bag.

Refrigerate fresh poultry and use within one or two days of purchase, or freeze it immediately, tightly wrapped in plastic wrap.

❖

TANDOORI CHICKEN BREAST SANDWICHES WITH YOGURT SAUCE

❖

Tandoor ovens are found throughout India and Indian restaurants worldwide. These brick and clay ovens with rounded tops are used to bake foods over direct heat from a smoky fire. With the right blend of yogurt and spices, the wonderful tandoori taste can be achieved right at home—even without a tandoor oven!

❖

12 ounces boneless skinless chicken breast halves (4 pieces)
1 tablespoon lemon juice
¼ cup plain nonfat yogurt
2 large garlic cloves, minced
1½ teaspoons finely chopped fresh ginger
¼ teaspoon ground cardamom
¼ teaspoon ground red pepper
Yogurt Sauce (page 32)
2 whole wheat pitas, cut into halves
½ cup grated carrot
½ cup finely shredded red cabbage
½ cup finely chopped red bell pepper

1 Lightly slash chicken breast halves 3 or 4 times with sharp knife. Place in medium bowl; sprinkle with lemon juice and toss to coat.

2 Combine yogurt, garlic, ginger, cardamom and ground red pepper in small bowl; add to chicken. Coat all pieces well with marinade; cover and refrigerate at least 1 hour or overnight.

3 Remove chicken from refrigerator 15 minutes before cooking. Preheat broiler. Prepare Yogurt Sauce; set aside.

4 Line broiler pan with foil. Arrange chicken on foil (do not let pieces touch) and brush with any remaining marinade. Broil 3 inches from heat about 5 to 6 minutes per side or until chicken is no longer pink in center.

5 Place one chicken breast half in each pita half with 2 tablespoons each of carrot, cabbage and bell pepper. Drizzle sandwiches with Yogurt Sauce. Garnish, if desired.

Makes 4 servings

(continued on page 32)

Tandoori Chicken Breast Sandwiches with Yogurt Sauce, continued

Nutrients per Serving:

Calories	211
(12% of calories from fat)	
Total Fat	3 g
Saturated Fat	1 g
Cholesterol	44 mg
Sodium	380 mg
Carbohydrate	25 g
Dietary Fiber	1 g
Protein	22 g
Calcium	113 mg
Iron	1 mg
Vitamin A	487 RE
Vitamin C	39 mg

DIETARY EXCHANGES:
1½ Starch/Bread, 2 Lean
Meat

YOGURT SAUCE

½ cup plain nonfat yogurt
2 teaspoons minced red onion
1 teaspoon minced cilantro
¼ teaspoon ground cumin
¼ teaspoon salt
   Dash ground red pepper

1 Blend all ingredients well in small bowl. Cover and refrigerate until ready to use.

Makes about ½ cup

❖

Cook's Tips

When purchasing fresh ginger, look for very firm pieces with smooth skin. Avoid ginger with protruding fibers and wrinkled skin, as these are sure signs of age.

To store fresh ginger, wrap in aluminum foil or paper towel and place in a plastic bag. Close the bag loosely and store in the refrigerator crisper drawer for up to one month.

❖

BALSAMIC CHICKEN

Nutrients per Serving:

Calories	174
(29% of calories from fat)	
Total Fat	5 g
Saturated Fat	1 g
Cholesterol	73 mg
Sodium	242 mg
Carbohydrate	3 g
Dietary Fiber	1 g
Protein	27 g
Calcium	18 mg
Iron	1 mg
Vitamin A	6 RE
Vitamin C	2 mg

DIETARY EXCHANGES:
3 Lean Meat

6 boneless skinless chicken breast halves
1½ teaspoons fresh rosemary leaves, minced *or* ½ teaspoon dried rosemary
2 cloves garlic, minced
¾ teaspoon pepper
½ teaspoon salt
1 tablespoon olive oil
¼ cup good-quality balsamic vinegar

1 Rinse chicken and pat dry. Combine rosemary, garlic, pepper and salt in small bowl; mix well. Place chicken in large bowl; drizzle chicken with oil and rub with spice mixture. Cover and refrigerate overnight.

2 Preheat oven to 450°F. Spray heavy roasting pan or iron skillet with nonstick cooking spray. Place chicken in pan; bake 10 minutes. Turn chicken over, stirring in 3 to 4 tablespoons water if drippings are beginning to stick to pan.

3 Bake about 10 minutes or until chicken is golden brown and no longer pink in center. If pan is dry, stir in another 1 to 2 tablespoons water to loosen drippings.

4 Drizzle balsamic vinegar over chicken in pan. Transfer chicken to plates. Stir liquid in pan; drizzle over chicken. Garnish, if desired. *Makes 6 servings*

❖

Cook's Tip
Heat and direct light cause herbs and spices to lose their flavors quickly. Store fresh herbs in the refrigerator, and dried herbs and spices in a dark, cool, dry place.

❖

POACHED TURKEY WITH ANCHO CHILI SAUCE

Ancho chilies are large dried chilies, about 3 to 4 inches long and deep reddish brown in color. Commonly used in sauces, these chilies have a spicy, smoky flavor that adds excitement to mild-flavored turkey.

❖

Nutrients per Serving:

Calories	291
(9% of calories from fat)	
Total Fat	3 g
Saturated Fat	1 g
Cholesterol	50 mg
Sodium	585 mg
Carbohydrate	39 g
Dietary Fiber	1 g
Protein	26 g
Calcium	49 mg
Iron	3 mg
Vitamin A	416 RE
Vitamin C	130 mg

DIETARY EXCHANGES:
2 Starch/Bread, 2½ Lean
Meat, 1 Vegetable

2 turkey tenderloins (½ pound each) *or* 1 pound boneless turkey breast
1 ancho chili pepper, seeded and stemmed
1¼ cups water
3 cloves garlic, peeled
1 cup roasted red peppers, coarsely chopped
1 teaspoon salt
½ teaspoon dried oregano leaves, crushed
3 cups cooked rice
4 green onions, finely chopped

1 Place turkey tenderloins in Dutch oven or stockpot; add enough water to cover. Bring to a boil over high heat.

2 Reduce heat to medium; cover and simmer 20 minutes or until turkey is no longer pink in center. Remove from Dutch oven; cover to keep warm. Let stand 15 minutes before slicing.

3 Meanwhile, combine ancho chili, 1¼ cups water and garlic in small saucepan; bring to a boil over high heat. Cover and turn off heat; let stand 15 minutes.

4 Add roasted red peppers, salt and oregano to chili mixture. Transfer mixture to food processor or blender; process until sauce is smooth.

5 Reserving 2 tablespoons green onion for garnish, combine rice and green onions. Arrange turkey over rice. Top with chili sauce and sprinkle with reserved green onion before serving. Garnish, if desired.

Makes 4 servings

CUBAN CHICKEN WITH PINEAPPLE

Choose pineapples with strong color and no signs of greening. The fruit should be slightly soft to the touch with firm green leaves and a sweet smell.

❖

¼ teaspoon salt
¼ teaspoon black pepper
¼ teaspoon dried oregano leaves, crushed
  Grated peel and juice of 1 lime
6 boneless skinless chicken breast halves
1 tablespoon olive oil, divided
1 medium onion, chopped
2 cloves garlic, minced
2 jalapeño peppers, seeded and chopped
2 cups chopped, seeded, peeled ripe tomatoes
1 cup ⅓-less-salt chicken broth
⅓ cup raisins
1 bay leaf
2 cups fresh pineapple tidbits
¼ cup rum

1 Combine salt, black pepper, oregano and lime peel in small bowl. Drizzle lime juice over chicken; sprinkle with seasoning mixture.

2 Heat 1½ teaspoons oil in large heavy skillet over medium-high heat. Add chicken; cover and cook about 10 minutes or until chicken is lightly browned on both sides. Transfer chicken to shallow baking dish with cover; arrange in single layer.

3 Preheat oven to 350°F. Heat remaining 1½ teaspoons oil in skillet. Add onion, garlic and jalapeños; cover and cook over medium heat about 5 minutes or until onion is tender, stirring occasionally. Stir in tomatoes, chicken broth, raisins and bay leaf; cook 5 minutes.

4 Pour onion mixture over chicken in baking dish. Cover and bake 20 minutes.

5 Meanwhile, combine pineapple and rum in small saucepan; cook over medium-high heat until most of liquid is evaporated. Uncover and spoon mixture over chicken; bake, uncovered, 10 minutes more. Garnish, if desired.

Makes 6 servings

Nutrients per Serving:

Calories	262
(20% of calories from fat)	
Total Fat	6 g
Saturated Fat	1 g
Cholesterol	73 mg
Sodium	166 mg
Carbohydrate	19 g
Dietary Fiber	2 g
Protein	28 g
Calcium	35 mg
Iron	2 mg
Vitamin A	55 RE
Vitamin C	29 mg

DIETARY EXCHANGES:
3 Lean Meat, 1 Fruit,
1 Vegetable

BEEF & PORK

THAI BEEF SALAD

❖

Flank steak should be sliced across the grain for tenderness. For best results, hold your knife at a 45° angle.

❖

Nutrients per Serving:

Calories	141
(26% of calories from fat)	
Total Fat	4 g
Saturated Fat	2 g
Cholesterol	27 mg
Sodium	238 mg
Carbohydrate	14 g
Dietary Fiber	3 g
Protein	13 g
Calcium	47 mg
Iron	2 mg
Vitamin A	2153 RE
Vitamin C	31 mg

DIETARY EXCHANGES:
1½ Lean Meat,
2 Vegetable

8 ounces beef flank steak
¼ cup low sodium soy sauce
2 jalapeño peppers, finely chopped
2 tablespoons packed brown sugar
1 clove garlic, minced
½ cup lime juice
6 green onions, thinly sliced
4 carrots, diagonally cut into thin slices
½ cup finely chopped fresh cilantro
6 romaine lettuce leaves

1 Place flank steak in resealable plastic food storage bag. Combine soy sauce, jalapeños, brown sugar and garlic in small bowl; mix well. Pour mixture over flank steak.

2 Close bag securely; turn to coat steak. Marinate in refrigerator 2 hours.

3 Preheat broiler. Drain steak; place on rack of broiler pan. Broil 4 inches from heat about 4 minutes per side or until desired doneness. Remove from heat; let rest 15 minutes.

4 Thinly slice steak across grain. Toss with lime juice, green onions, carrots and cilantro in large bowl. Serve salad immediately on lettuce leaves. Garnish with chives and radish flowers, if desired.

Makes 4 servings

BARBECUED PORK SANDWICHES

This simple recipe is terrific for entertaining—it's a can't-miss crowd pleaser that's fast, healthy and delicious. The pork tenderloins can be baked with the barbecue sauce in advance, then the sandwiches can be quickly assembled at party time.

2 pork tenderloins (about 1½ pounds total)
⅓ cup prepared barbecue sauce
½ cup prepared horseradish
4 pita bread rounds, cut into halves
1 onion, thinly sliced
4 romaine lettuce leaves
1 red bell pepper, cut lengthwise into ¼-inch-thick slices
1 green bell pepper, cut lengthwise into ¼-inch-thick slices

1 Preheat oven to 400°F. Place pork tenderloins in roasting pan; brush with barbecue sauce.

2 Bake tenderloins 15 minutes; turn and bake 10 minutes or until internal temperature reaches 155°F. Cover with foil; let stand 10 minutes.

3 Slice pork across grain. Spread horseradish on pita bread halves; stuff with pork, onion, lettuce and bell peppers. Garnish, if desired.

Makes 4 servings

Nutrients per Serving:

Calories	440
(17% of calories from fat)	
Total Fat	9 g
Saturated Fat	2 g
Cholesterol	121 mg
Sodium	628 mg
Carbohydrate	46 g
Dietary Fiber	2 g
Protein	46 g
Calcium	61 mg
Iron	3 mg
Vitamin A	185 RE
Vitamin C	66 mg

DIETARY EXCHANGES:
2½ Starch/Bread, 4 Lean Meat, 1 Vegetable

Cook's Tip
Use any leftover pork as the base for a main-course salad, adding vegetables, pasta or rice and a low fat dressing for a quick and hearty meal.

HEARTY HUNGARIAN GOULASH

❖

Goulash is a Hungarian stew made with beef, vegetables and paprika. Americans are most familiar with a mild Spanish paprika, while Hungarian paprika is a much stronger, hotter spice and is preferred in most recipes. Paprika is the only known dry source of vitamin C, with one tablespoon said to equal the juice of four lemons!

❖

1 pound beef round steak
1 teaspoon canola oil
1 onion, chopped
3 cloves garlic, minced
2 teaspoons paprika
2 teaspoons caraway seeds
¾ cup water
2 carrots, cut crosswise into ¼-inch-thick slices
1 large red potato, peeled and cut into ½-inch cubes
1 teaspoon hot pepper sauce
1 cup nonfat sour cream
1 teaspoon salt
1 pound yolk-free egg noodles, cooked according to package directions

1 Trim fat from round steak. Cut steak into ¾-inch pieces; set aside.

2 Heat oil in large skillet over medium heat. Add onion, garlic, paprika and caraway seeds; cook 5 to 7 minutes, stirring occasionally. Stir in water, carrots, potato and hot pepper sauce; cover and cook 15 minutes or until vegetables are tender.

3 Meanwhile, spray medium skillet with nonstick cooking spray; heat over medium heat. Add steak; cook and stir about 4 minutes or until just beginning to brown. Add to vegetable mixture; cook 5 minutes, stirring occasionally.

4 Stir in sour cream and salt; cook over medium-low heat until heated through. Serve over egg noodles. Garnish with fresh parsley, if desired.   *Makes 6 servings*

Nutrients per Serving:

Calories	447
(14% of calories from fat)	
Total Fat	7 g
Saturated Fat	2 g
Cholesterol	48 mg
Sodium	442 mg
Carbohydrate	64 g
Dietary Fiber	4 g
Protein	32 g
Calcium	88 mg
Iron	4 mg
Vitamin A	881 RE
Vitamin C	8 mg

DIETARY EXCHANGES:
4 Starch/Bread, 2½ Lean Meat, 1 Vegetable

JERKED PORK CHOPS

Spice rubs are a traditional method of adding sweet and savory flavors to meats and poultry. This way of cooking has been used on the Caribbean islands for years but is just being rediscovered here for its health value: lots of flavor without a lot of fat.

2 teaspoons onion powder
1 teaspoon sugar
1 teaspoon dried thyme leaves, crushed
½ teaspoon salt
½ teaspoon ground allspice
½ teaspoon ground red pepper
¼ teaspoon ground nutmeg
4 boneless pork loin chops, trimmed of fat
4 cups cooked white rice
2 green onions, finely chopped

1 Combine onion powder, sugar, thyme, salt, allspice, ground red pepper and nutmeg in small bowl; mix well. Rub pork chops on both sides with spice mixture.

2 Spray nonstick skillet with nonstick cooking spray; heat over medium heat. Cook pork chops about 5 minutes per side or until juicy and barely pink in center.

3 Serve pork chops over rice; sprinkle with green onions. Garnish with red onion and geranium leaf, if desired.

Makes 4 servings

Cook's Tip
Make up a double or triple batch of jerk seasoning to have on hand; it can be stored in an airtight glass jar for weeks. Try it on chicken breasts for a change of pace.

Nutrients per Serving:

Calories	385
(26% of calories from fat)	
Total Fat	11 g
Saturated Fat	4 g
Cholesterol	63 mg
Sodium	318 mg
Carbohydrate	47 g
Dietary Fiber	<1 g
Protein	23 g
Calcium	37 mg
Iron	3 mg
Vitamin A	25 RE
Vitamin C	2 mg

DIETARY EXCHANGES:
3 Starch/Bread, 3 Lean Meat

DEVILED BURGERS

2 slices bread, finely chopped
¼ cup finely chopped onion
¼ cup tomato ketchup
1 tablespoon Worcestershire sauce
2 teaspoons prepared mustard
2 teaspoons creamy horseradish
½ teaspoon garlic powder
½ teaspoon chili powder
1 pound extra-lean ground beef
6 hamburger buns

1 Preheat broiler. Combine bread, onion, ketchup, Worcestershire sauce, mustard, horseradish, garlic powder and chili powder in large bowl until well blended. Gently blend ground beef into mixture. (*Do not overwork.*)

2 Shape mixture into 6 (3-inch) burgers. Place burgers on ungreased jelly-roll pan.

3 Broil burgers 4 inches from heat source 4 minutes per side or until desired doneness. Serve on hamburger buns. Garnish, if desired. *Makes 6 servings*

Nutrients per Serving:

Calories	298
(29% of calories from fat)	
Total Fat	9 g
Saturated Fat	3 g
Cholesterol	50 mg
Sodium	519 mg
Carbohydrate	30 g
Dietary Fiber	1 g
Protein	22 g
Calcium	85 mg
Iron	4 mg
Vitamin A	23 RE
Vitamin C	7 mg

DIETARY EXCHANGES:
2 Starch/Bread, 2 Lean Meat, 1 Fat

❖

Cook's Tip

You can store ground beef for up to 2 days in the refrigerator or up to 6 months in the freezer. Choose coarsely ground beef to provide the best texture for hamburgers.

❖

GRILLED PORK TENDERLOIN WITH APPLE SALSA

❖❖

Lean pork is a terrific source of protein, B vitamins and zinc. As the leanest cut of pork, tenderloin has only 133 calories and 4 grams of fat in a 3-ounce serving; it also adapts well to a wide variety of flavors and cooking methods. Here the pork may be grilled outside on a gas or charcoal grill or inside on a stovetop grill.

❖❖

1 tablespoon chili powder
½ teaspoon garlic powder
1 pound pork tenderloin
2 Granny Smith apples, peeled, cored and finely chopped
1 can (4 ounces) chopped green chilies
¼ cup lemon juice
3 tablespoons finely chopped fresh cilantro
1 clove garlic, minced
1 teaspoon dried oregano leaves, crushed
½ teaspoon salt

1 Spray grid well with nonstick cooking spray. Preheat grill to medium-high heat.

2 Combine chili powder and garlic powder in small bowl; mix well. Coat pork with spice mixture.

3 Grill pork 30 minutes, turning occasionally, until internal temperature reaches 155°F when tested with meat thermometer in thickest part of tenderloin. Cover with foil and let rest 10 minutes before slicing.

4 To make apple salsa, combine apples, chilies, lemon juice, cilantro, garlic, oregano and salt in medium bowl; mix well.

5 Slice pork across grain; serve with salsa. Garnish, if desired.   *Makes 4 servings*

Nutrients per Serving:

Calories	201
(21% of calories from fat)	
Total Fat	5 g
Saturated Fat	1 g
Cholesterol	81 mg
Sodium	678 mg
Carbohydrate	14 g
Dietary Fiber	2 g
Protein	26 g
Calcium	30 mg
Iron	2 mg
Vitamin A	101 RE
Vitamin C	31 mg

DIETARY EXCHANGES:
3 Lean Meat, ½ Fruit

GRILLED FLANK STEAK WITH HORSERADISH SAUCE

Prepared horseradish is combined with nonfat sour cream to lighten up a classic sauce. Purchase horseradish in small quantities, as it begins to turn bitter and lose its hotness within four weeks after opening.

1 pound beef flank steak
2 tablespoons low sodium soy sauce
1 tablespoon red wine vinegar
2 cloves garlic, minced
½ teaspoon pepper
1 cup nonfat sour cream
1 tablespoon prepared horseradish
1 tablespoon Dijon mustard
¼ cup finely chopped fresh parsley
½ teaspoon salt
6 sourdough rolls, split
6 romaine lettuce leaves

1 Place flank steak in large resealable plastic food storage bag. Add soy sauce, vinegar, garlic and pepper. Close bag securely; turn to coat. Marinate in refrigerator at least 1 hour.

2 Prepare grill or preheat broiler. Drain steak; discard marinade. Grill or broil over medium-high heat 5 minutes. Turn beef; grill 6 minutes for medium-rare or until desired doneness. Cover with foil; let stand 15 minutes. Thinly slice steak across grain.

3 Combine sour cream, horseradish, mustard, parsley and salt in small bowl until well blended. Spread rolls with horseradish sauce; layer with sliced steak and lettuce. Garnish with small pickles, if desired.

Makes 6 servings

Nutrients per Serving:

Calories 220
(27% of calories from fat)
Total Fat 6 g
Saturated Fat 3 g
Cholesterol 35 mg
Sodium 542 mg
Carbohydrate 20 g
Dietary Fiber <1 g
Protein 20 g
Calcium 93 mg
Iron 3 mg
Vitamin A 216 RE
Vitamin C 9 mg

DIETARY EXCHANGES:
1 Starch/Bread, 2½ Lean Meat

GUEST CHECK

CHECK NUMBER
4948

SERVER
3

TABLE
4

SEAFOOD

SOUTHERN BREADED CATFISH

❖

Southern cooks have traditionally breaded and deep-fried catfish. This new version retains the crunchy, flavorful coating but browns the fillets in a skillet to significantly reduce the amount of fat in the dish.

❖

⅓ cup pecan halves
¼ cup cornmeal
2 tablespoons all-purpose flour
1 teaspoon paprika
¼ teaspoon ground red pepper
2 egg whites
4 catfish fillets (about 1 pound)
4 cups cooked rice

1 Place pecans in food processor or blender; process until finely chopped. Combine pecans, cornmeal, flour, paprika and ground red pepper in shallow bowl.

2 Beat egg whites in small bowl with wire whisk until foamy. Dip catfish fillets in pecan mixture, then in egg whites, then again in pecan mixture. Place fillets on plate; cover and refrigerate at least 15 minutes.

3 Spray large nonstick skillet with nonstick cooking spray; heat over medium-high heat. Place catfish fillets in single layer in skillet.

4 Cook fillets 2 minutes per side or until golden brown. Serve over rice. Serve with vegetables and garnish, if desired. *Makes 4 servings*

Nutrients per Serving:

Calories	297
(25% of calories from fat)	
Total Fat	8 g
Saturated Fat	1 g
Cholesterol	65 mg
Sodium	76 mg
Carbohydrate	33 g
Dietary Fiber	2 g
Protein	22 g
Calcium	24 mg
Iron	2 mg
Vitamin A	54 RE
Vitamin C	1 mg

DIETARY EXCHANGES:
2 Starch/Bread, 2½ Lean Meat, ½ Fat

GRILLED SCALLOPS AND VEGETABLES WITH CILANTRO SAUCE

❖

Also known as coriander or Chinese parsley, cilantro contributes a burst of lemon-peppery flavor and a good supply of Vitamin C to this dish. Store cilantro, stems down, in a glass of water in the refrigerator with a plastic bag over the leaves to prevent drying. Use only the leaves in cooking and tear them just before using to maximize flavor and nutritional content.

❖

Nutrients per Serving:	
Calories	171
(21% of calories from fat)	
Total Fat	4 g
Saturated Fat	<1 g
Cholesterol	48 mg
Sodium	258 mg
Carbohydrate	11 g
Dietary Fiber	3 g
Protein	24 g
Calcium	162 mg
Iron	4 mg
Vitamin A	102 RE
Vitamin C	15 mg

DIETARY EXCHANGES:
3 Lean Meat, 1 Vegetable

1 teaspoon hot chili oil
1 teaspoon Oriental sesame oil
1 green onion, chopped
1 tablespoon finely chopped fresh ginger
1 cup ⅓-less-salt chicken broth
1 cup chopped fresh cilantro
1 pound sea scallops
2 medium zucchini, cut into ½-inch slices
2 medium yellow squash, cut into ½-inch slices
1 medium yellow onion, cut into wedges
8 large mushrooms

1 Spray cold grid with nonstick cooking spray. Preheat grill to medium-high heat. Heat chili oil and sesame oil in small saucepan over medium-low heat. Add green onion; cook about 15 seconds or just until fragrant. Add ginger; cook 1 minute.

2 Add chicken broth; bring mixture to a boil. Cook until liquid is reduced by half. Place mixture in blender or food processor with cilantro; blend until smooth. Set aside.

3 Thread scallops and vegetables onto skewers. Grill about 8 minutes per side or until scallops turn opaque. Serve hot with cilantro sauce. Garnish, if desired.

Makes 4 servings

❖

Cook's Tip

Sea scallops are less expensive and more widely available than the smaller bay scallops. If you prefer bay scallops, adjust the cooking time accordingly, as they cook very quickly and toughen when overcooked.

❖

SHRIMP CURRY

1¼ pounds raw large shrimp
1 large onion, chopped
½ cup canned light coconut milk
3 cloves garlic, minced
2 tablespoons finely chopped fresh ginger
2 to 3 teaspoons hot curry powder
¼ teaspoon salt
1 can (14½ ounces) diced tomatoes
1 teaspoon cornstarch
2 tablespoons chopped fresh cilantro
3 cups hot cooked rice

1 Peel shrimp, leaving tails attached and reserving shells. Place shells in large saucepan; cover with water. Bring to a boil over high heat. Reduce heat to low; simmer 15 to 20 minutes. Strain shrimp stock and set aside. Discard shells.

2 Spray large skillet with nonstick cooking spray; heat over medium heat. Add onion; cover and cook 5 minutes. Add coconut milk, garlic, ginger, curry powder, salt and ½ cup shrimp stock; bring to a boil. Reduce heat to low and simmer 10 to 15 minutes or until onion is tender.

3 Add shrimp and tomatoes to skillet; return mixture to a simmer. Cook 3 minutes.

4 Stir cornstarch into 1 tablespoon cooled shrimp stock until dissolved. Add mixture to skillet with cilantro; simmer 1 to 2 minutes or just until slightly thickened, stirring occasionally. Serve over rice. Garnish with carrot and lime slices, if desired.

Makes 6 servings

Nutrients per Serving:

Calories	219
(10% of calories from fat)	
Total Fat	2 g
Saturated Fat	<1 g
Cholesterol	145 mg
Sodium	369 mg
Carbohydrate	30 g
Dietary Fiber	1 g
Protein	19 g
Calcium	68 mg
Iron	4 mg
Vitamin A	104 RE
Vitamin C	15 mg

DIETARY EXCHANGES:
1½ Starch/Bread, 2 Lean Meat, 1 Vegetable

MUSTARD-GRILLED RED SNAPPER

Red snapper is a mild-flavored, low fat fish. The fat that fish does contain is known as omega-3 fatty acid, thought to provide a wide range of health benefits. Try jazzing up red snapper with this tangy mustard coating before grilling it. Fish is done when it is opaque and just begins to flake easily when tested with a fork.

½ cup Dijon mustard
1 tablespoon red wine vinegar
1 teaspoon ground red pepper
4 red snapper fillets (about 1½ pounds)

1 Spray cold grid or broiling rack with nonstick cooking spray. Prepare grill or preheat broiler.

2 Combine mustard, vinegar and ground red pepper in small bowl; mix well. Coat fish fillets thoroughly with mustard mixture.

3 Grill fish over medium-high heat or broil about 4 minutes per side or until fish flakes easily when tested with fork. Garnish with fresh Italian parsley and red peppercorns, if desired. Serve immediately.

Makes 4 servings

Nutrients per Serving:

Calories	200
(20% of calories from fat)	
Total Fat	4 g
Saturated Fat	1 g
Cholesterol	62 mg
Sodium	477 mg
Carbohydrate	2 g
Dietary Fiber	<1 g
Protein	37 g
Calcium	92 mg
Iron	1 mg
Vitamin A	19 RE
Vitamin C	<1 mg

DIETARY EXCHANGES:
3½ Lean Meat

Cook's Tip
When purchasing fresh fish, look for fish that are firm and resilient to the touch. The fish should smell fresh and clean, not fishy, and have clear eyes, intact scales and vibrant red- or pink-colored gills.

CAJUN-STYLE CORN WITH CRAYFISH

This dish is an old Southern favorite known as maque choux *in South Louisiana. If crayfish are not readily available in your area, use shrimp instead. Or, leave out the seafood entirely and enjoy a deliciously different side dish.*

Nutrients per Serving:

Calories	262
(15% of calories from fat)	
Total Fat	5 g
Saturated Fat	1 g
Cholesterol	125 mg
Sodium	631 mg
Carbohydrate	38 g
Dietary Fiber	5 g
Protein	22 g
Calcium	62 mg
Iron	2 mg
Vitamin A	75 RE
Vitamin C	32 mg

DIETARY EXCHANGES:
2 Starch/Bread,
½ Vegetable

6 ears corn on the cob
1 tablespoon vegetable oil
1 medium onion, chopped
½ cup chopped green bell pepper
½ cup chopped red bell pepper
1 cup water
1 teaspoon salt
⅛ teaspoon black pepper
⅛ teaspoon ground red pepper
¾ pound crayfish tail meat

1 Cut corn from cobs in two or three layers so that kernels are not left whole. Scrape cobs to remove remaining juice and pulp.

2 Heat oil in large skillet over medium heat. Add onion and bell peppers; cook 5 minutes, stirring occasionally. Add corn, water, salt, black pepper and ground red pepper; bring to a boil. Reduce heat to low; simmer 10 to 15 minutes.

3 Add crayfish; return mixture to a simmer. Cook 3 to 5 minutes or just until crayfish turn opaque. Garnish, if desired.

Makes 6 servings

Cook's Tip

To remove corn kernels from the cob, first cut a small piece from the tip so the cob will stand flat. Stand the cob upright on its flat end and use a sharp knife to cut downward, removing 3 or 4 rows of kernels at a time.

GRAINS & MORE

VEGETARIAN PAELLA

This colorful Spanish dish is named for the special shallow two-handled pan in which it is traditionally prepared and served.

1 tablespoon olive oil
1 medium onion, chopped
1 serrano pepper, finely chopped
1 red bell pepper, diced
1 green bell pepper, diced
3 cloves garlic, minced
½ teaspoon saffron threads, crushed
½ teaspoon paprika
1 cup uncooked long-grain white rice
3 cups water
1 can (15 ounces) chick-peas (garbanzo beans), rinsed and drained
14 ounces artichoke hearts in water, drained, cut into halves
1 cup frozen green peas
1½ teaspoons grated lemon peel

1 Preheat oven to 375°F. Heat oil in large paella pan or heavy, ovenproof skillet over medium-high heat. Add onion, serrano pepper and bell peppers; cook and stir about 7 minutes.

2 Add garlic, saffron and paprika; cook 3 minutes. Add rice; cook and stir 1 minute. Add water, chick-peas, artichoke hearts, green peas and lemon peel; mix well.

3 Cover and bake 25 minutes or until rice is tender. Garnish with fresh bay leaves and lemon slices, if desired.

Makes 6 servings

Nutrients per Serving:

Calories	462
(12% of calories from fat)	
Total Fat	6 g
Saturated Fat	<1 g
Cholesterol	0 mg
Sodium	107 mg
Carbohydrate	84 g
Dietary Fiber	5 g
Protein	21 g
Calcium	172 mg
Iron	8 mg
Vitamin A	132 RE
Vitamin C	55 mg

DIETARY EXCHANGES:
5 Starch/Bread,
2 Vegetable, 1 Fat

SPICY VEGETABLE CHILI

Wheat berries are whole, unprocessed kernels of wheat that add a slight crunch to the chili, in addition to a good amount of protein and B vitamins.

❖

Nutrients per Serving:

Calories	409
(8% of calories from fat)	
Total Fat	4 g
Saturated Fat	<1 g
Cholesterol	0 mg
Sodium	711 mg
Carbohydrate	86 g
Dietary Fiber	18 g
Protein	19 g
Calcium	140 mg
Iron	6 mg
Vitamin A	155 RE
Vitamin C	85 mg

DIETARY EXCHANGES:
3 Starch/Bread, 1½ Fruit,
2 Vegetable

½ cup uncooked wheat berries
1 large onion, chopped
½ green bell pepper, chopped
½ yellow or red bell pepper, chopped
2 ribs celery, sliced
3 cloves garlic, minced
1 can (14½ ounces) chopped tomatoes
1 can (15 ounces) red kidney beans, rinsed and drained
1 can (15 ounces) chick-peas (garbanzo beans), rinsed and drained
¾ cup raisins
½ cup water
1 tablespoon chili con carne seasoning or chili powder
1 teaspoon dried oregano leaves, crushed
1 tablespoon chopped fresh parsley
1½ teaspoons hot pepper sauce

1 Place wheat berries in small saucepan and cover with 2 cups water; let soak overnight. Bring to a boil over high heat. Reduce heat to low; cover and cook 45 minutes to 1 hour or until wheat berries are tender. Drain; set aside.

2 Spray large skillet or saucepan with nonstick cooking spray; heat over medium heat. Add onion; cover and cook 5 minutes. Add bell peppers, celery and garlic; cover and cook 5 minutes, stirring occasionally.

3 Add tomatoes, kidney beans, chick-peas, raisins, ½ cup water, chili seasoning, oregano and wheat berries to skillet; mix well. Bring to a boil over high heat. Reduce heat to low; simmer 25 to 30 minutes, stirring occasionally. Just before serving, stir in parsley and hot pepper sauce. Garnish, if desired. *Makes 4 servings*

SOUTH-OF-THE-BORDER PIZZA

❖

A vibrant red-, yellow- and green-topped pizza is a colorful and delicious way to incorporate vegetables into your diet. If one jalapeño doesn't provide enough heat, sprinkle the pizza with red pepper flakes after baking.

❖

1 prepared pizza shell or crust (about 12 inches)
1 cup cooked low sodium kidney beans, rinsed and drained
1 cup frozen whole kernel corn, thawed
1 tomato, chopped
¼ cup finely chopped fresh cilantro
1 jalapeño pepper, finely chopped
¼ cup (4 ounces) shredded reduced fat Monterey Jack cheese

1 Preheat oven to 450°F. Place pizza shell on ungreased pizza pan or baking sheet.

2 Arrange beans, corn, tomato, cilantro and jalapeño over pizza shell. Sprinkle evenly with cheese.

3 Bake pizza 8 to 10 minutes or until cheese is melted and lightly browned. Garnish with green bell pepper, if desired. *Makes 4 servings*

Nutrients per Serving:

Calories	361
(19% of calories from fat)	
Total Fat	7 g
Saturated Fat	3 g
Cholesterol	20 mg
Sodium	569 mg
Carbohydrate	53 g
Dietary Fiber	4 g
Protein	20 g
Calcium	281 mg
Iron	4 mg
Vitamin A	103 RE
Vitamin C	14 mg

DIETARY EXCHANGES:
3 Starch/Bread, 1 Lean Meat, 2 Vegetable, 1 Fat

❖

Cook's Tip

For an extra Mexican touch, use a large flour tortilla instead of a prepared pizza crust. Prepare and bake as directed above, or top with another tortilla and enjoy a South-of-the-Border Quesadilla instead.

❖

COUSCOUS WITH CHICK-PEAS AND VEGETABLES

Every kitchen should have couscous on hand—it makes a great main dish or side dish and it only takes 5 minutes to cook!

❖

Nutrients per Serving:

Calories	324
(7% of calories from fat)	
Total Fat	2 g
Saturated Fat	<1 g
Cholesterol	0 mg
Sodium	330 mg
Carbohydrate	63 g
Dietary Fiber	9 g
Protein	14 g
Calcium	112 mg
Iron	4 mg
Vitamin A	504 RE
Vitamin C	22 mg

DIETARY EXCHANGES:
4 Starch/Bread,
1 Vegetable, ½ Fat

1 cup dried chick-peas (garbanzo beans)
2 cans (14 ounces each) ⅓-less-salt chicken broth
1 large onion, quartered and sliced
2 large cloves garlic, minced
1 teaspoon ground cinnamon
1 teaspoon red pepper flakes
½ teaspoon paprika
½ teaspoon saffron or turmeric (optional)
½ teaspoon salt
½ pound eggplant, cut into ¾-inch cubes
1 large sweet potato, peeled and cut into ¾-inch cubes
¾ pound zucchini, cut into ¾-inch cubes
1 can (14½ ounces) chopped tomatoes
2 tablespoons finely chopped fresh parsley
2 tablespoons finely chopped fresh cilantro
4 cups hot cooked couscous, cooked without salt

1 Sort and rinse chick-peas. Cover with water and let soak overnight; drain. Place in Dutch oven with chicken broth; bring to a boil over high heat.

2 Add onion, garlic, cinnamon, red pepper flakes, paprika and saffron; reduce heat to low. Cover and simmer 1 hour or until beans are tender. Stir in salt.

3 Add eggplant and sweet potato; cook 10 minutes. Add zucchini and tomatoes; cook 10 minutes or just until all vegetables are tender. Stir in parsley and cilantro; spoon mixture over hot couscous. Garnish with sweet potato slices and chives, if desired.

Makes 6 servings

SPICY SESAME NOODLES

❖

Soba is a Japanese noodle made from buckwheat flour with a different taste and texture from the kind of spaghetti familiar to most Americans. Noodles of all sorts are extremely popular in Japan, eaten in soups or with sauces and with a great deal of noise. Eating noodles quietly is considered insulting—so slurp loudly and enjoy!

❖

Nutrients per Serving:

Calories	145
(23% of calories from fat)	
Total Fat	4 g
Saturated Fat	1 g
Cholesterol	0 mg
Sodium	358 mg
Carbohydrate	24 g
Dietary Fiber	1 g
Protein	6 g
Calcium	22 mg
Iron	1 mg
Vitamin A	156 RE
Vitamin C	47 mg

DIETARY EXCHANGES:
1½ Starch/Bread,
½ Vegetable, ½ Fat

6 ounces uncooked dry soba (buckwheat) noodles
2 teaspoons sesame oil
1 tablespoon sesame seeds
½ cup ⅓-less-salt chicken broth
1 tablespoon creamy peanut butter
½ cup thinly sliced green onions
½ cup minced red bell pepper
4 teaspoons light soy sauce
1½ teaspoons finely chopped, seeded jalapeño pepper
1 clove garlic, minced
¼ teaspoon red pepper flakes

1 Cook noodles according to package directions. (Do not overcook.) Rinse noodles thoroughly with cold water to stop cooking and remove salty residue; drain. Place noodles in large bowl; toss with sesame oil.

2 Place sesame seeds in small skillet. Cook over medium heat about 3 minutes or until seeds begin to pop and turn golden brown, stirring frequently. Remove from heat; set aside.

3 Combine chicken broth and peanut butter in small bowl with wire whisk until blended. (Mixture may look curdled.) Stir in green onions, red bell pepper, soy sauce, jalapeño, garlic and red pepper flakes.

4 Pour mixture over noodles; toss to coat. Cover and let stand 30 minutes at room temperature or refrigerate up to 24 hours. Sprinkle with toasted sesame seeds before serving. Garnish, if desired. *Makes 6 servings*

MEXICAN HOT POT

❖

The word "pinto" is Spanish for paint, explaining the theory that pinto beans were so named because their mottled beige appearance before cooking looks like they were dabbed with paint. Cooked pinto beans add a pretty pink color and hearty texture to this vegetarian stew.

❖

1 tablespoon canola oil
1 onion, sliced
3 cloves garlic, minced
2 teaspoons red pepper flakes
2 teaspoons dried oregano leaves, crushed
1 teaspoon ground cumin
1 can (28 ounces) tomatoes, chopped
1 can (15 ounces) chick-peas (garbanzo beans), rinsed and drained
1 can (15 ounces) pinto beans, rinsed and drained
2 cups whole kernel corn, fresh or frozen
1 cup water
6 cups shredded iceberg lettuce

1 Heat oil in stockpot or Dutch oven over medium-high heat. Add onion and garlic; cook and stir 5 minutes. Add red pepper flakes, oregano and cumin; mix well.

2 Stir in tomatoes, chick-peas, pinto beans, corn and water; bring to a boil over high heat.

3 Reduce heat to medium-low; cover and simmer 15 minutes. Top individual servings with 1 cup shredded lettuce. Serve hot.   *Makes 6 servings*

Nutrients per Serving:

Calories	252
(16% of calories from fat)	
Total Fat	5 g
Saturated Fat	<1 g
Cholesterol	0 mg
Sodium	765 mg
Carbohydrate	46 g
Dietary Fiber	7 g
Protein	12 g
Calcium	93 mg
Iron	4 mg
Vitamin A	142 RE
Vitamin C	29 mg

DIETARY EXCHANGES:
3 Starch/Bread, 1 Vegetable, ½ Fat

❖

Cook's Tip

For a heartier meat lover's hot pot, brown some ground beef or chunks of chicken with the onion and garlic; cook until the meat is no longer pink.

❖

VEGETABLES & SIDES

WARM ROASTED VEGETABLE SALAD

Roasting vegetables brings out their natural sweetness. It's an easy cooking method that works well with a variety of vegetables—try eggplants, squash, potatoes and other root vegetables (cooking times will vary).

4 cups broccoli florets
2 red bell peppers, cut into ¼-inch-thick slices
1 small red onion, cut into ¼-inch-thick slices
1 small yellow onion, cut into ¼-inch-thick slices
1½ teaspoons olive oil
1 tablespoon Dijon mustard
1 tablespoon balsamic vinegar
1 teaspoon hot pepper sauce
½ teaspoon salt
¼ cup slivered fresh basil

1 Preheat oven to 350°F. Combine broccoli, bell peppers, onions and oil in large casserole dish; toss to coat.

2 Bake vegetables 25 minutes, stirring occasionally.

3 Meanwhile, combine mustard, vinegar, hot pepper sauce and salt in small bowl with wire whisk until smooth. Stir mixture into hot vegetables; toss to coat. Sprinkle salad with basil; garnish, if desired. Serve warm. *Makes 6 servings*

Nutrients per Serving:

Calories	50
(25% of calories from fat)	
Total Fat	2 g
Saturated Fat	<1 g
Cholesterol	0 mg
Sodium	8 mg
Carbohydrate	8 g
Dietary Fiber	3 g
Protein	3 g
Calcium	44 mg
Iron	1 mg
Vitamin A	249 RE
Vitamin C	114 mg

DIETARY EXCHANGES:
1½ Vegetable

BAKED CORN TIMBALES

❖

This recipe is baked in ramekins, which are individually sized baking dishes. Any other small ovenproof ceramic or glass dishes may be used instead, creating a welcome change from having plain vegetables with your meals.

❖

6 sun-dried tomatoes (not packed in oil)
2 whole eggs
2 egg whites
2 cups frozen whole kernel corn, thawed
¾ cup evaporated skimmed milk
1 teaspoon salt
1 teaspoon dry mustard
1 teaspoon hot pepper sauce

1 Preheat oven to 350°F. Spray 6 (6-ounce) ramekins or small ovenproof dishes with nonstick cooking spray.

2 To reconstitute sun-dried tomatoes, place in small bowl and cover with hot water. Let stand 15 minutes. Drain and finely chop.

3 Beat whole eggs and egg whites in medium bowl with wire whisk until frothy. Fold in tomatoes, corn, milk, salt, mustard and hot pepper sauce until well combined. Fill ramekins ¾ full with mixture.

4 Place ramekins in large roasting pan; pour hot water around ramekins to depth of about ½ inch. Bake 35 minutes or until set and lightly browned. Invert ramekins onto serving plate to release timbales. Garnish with additional corn and red bell pepper strips, if desired. Serve immediately.

Makes 6 servings

Nutrients per Serving:	
Calories	128
(13% of calories from fat)	
Total Fat	2 g
Saturated Fat	1 g
Cholesterol	72 mg
Sodium	449 mg
Carbohydrate	22 g
Dietary Fiber	2 g
Protein	9 g
Calcium	120 mg
Iron	1 mg
Vitamin A	569 RE
Vitamin C	12 mg

DIETARY EXCHANGES:
1 Starch/Bread, ½ Lean Meat, 1 Vegetable

❖

Cook's Tip

Evaporated skimmed milk can be stored at room temperature until opened. After opening, the canned milk should be stored in a tightly covered container in the refrigerator for no more than one week.

❖

SPICY ORIENTAL GREEN BEANS

❖

Crisp, crunchy, low-calorie green beans make a super side dish, especially when given an Asian flair. Chili sauce with garlic is a boldly flavored condiment found in Oriental grocery stores; a pinch of ground red pepper can also be used.

❖

1 pound whole green beans, trimmed
2 tablespoons chopped green onion
2 tablespoons dry sherry or chicken broth
1½ tablespoons low sodium soy sauce
1 teaspoon chili sauce with garlic
1 teaspoon Oriental sesame oil
1 clove garlic, minced

1 Fill Dutch oven with water to depth of ½ inch. Bring water to a boil. Place green beans in steamer basket; place basket in Dutch oven. Cover and steam beans about 5 minutes or just until crisp-tender. Drain and set aside.

2 Combine green onion, sherry, soy sauce, chili sauce, sesame oil and garlic in small bowl.

3 Spray large skillet with nonstick cooking spray; heat over medium heat. Add green beans; pour soy sauce mixture over beans. Toss well to coat. Cook 3 to 5 minutes, stirring constantly until heated through. Garnish with edible flowers, such as pansies, violets or nasturtiums, if desired.

Makes 4 servings

Nutrients per Serving:

Calories	54
(19% of calories from fat)	
Total Fat	1 g
Saturated Fat	<1 g
Cholesterol	0 mg
Sodium	218 mg
Carbohydrate	8 g
Dietary Fiber	<1 g
Protein	2 g
Calcium	55 mg
Iron	1 mg
Vitamin A	72 RE
Vitamin C	11 mg

DIETARY EXCHANGES:
2 Vegetable

❖

Cook's Tip

Fresh green beans should be firm, smooth and brightly colored. They should be crisp enough to snap when bent in half.

❖

ROAST CAJUN POTATOES

Potatoes are a wonderful comfort food—not just because they taste great but also because they provide many terrific health benefits. Low in calories and high in vitamin C, potassium and fiber, potatoes are a smart choice for dinner—and always a popular one!

1 pound russet potatoes
2 tablespoons finely chopped fresh parsley
2 teaspoons canola oil
½ teaspoon garlic powder
½ teaspoon onion powder
½ teaspoon ground red pepper
½ teaspoon dried thyme leaves, crushed
¼ teaspoon black pepper

1 Preheat oven to 400°F. Peel potatoes; cut each potato lengthwise into 8 wedges. Place on ungreased jelly-roll pan.

2 Toss potatoes with parsley, oil, garlic powder, onion powder, ground red pepper, thyme and black pepper until evenly coated.

3 Bake 50 minutes, turning wedges halfway through cooking time. Serve immediately. Garnish, if desired.

Makes 4 servings

Nutrients per Serving:

Calories	120
(18% of calories from fat)	
Total Fat	2 g
Saturated Fat	<1 g
Cholesterol	0 mg
Sodium	7 mg
Carbohydrate	23 g
Dietary Fiber	2 g
Protein	2 g
Calcium	17 mg
Iron	1 mg
Vitamin A	20 RE
Vitamin C	11 mg

DIETARY EXCHANGES:
1½ Starch/Bread, ½ Fat

❖

Cook's Tip
The best potatoes for baking are the starchy or mealy varieties, such as russet or Idaho. Look for dry, well-shaped potatoes without sprouting and without any greenish tint that may indicate too much exposure to light.

❖

JALAPEÑO COLE SLAW

This light and spicy new twist on an old favorite has no added fat. Allow several hours for marinating or make the salad a day ahead and refrigerate it. Hot and sweet, this slaw is perfect for picnics; serve alongside sandwiches, burgers or grilled chicken.

6 cups preshredded cabbage or coleslaw mix
2 tomatoes, seeded and chopped
6 green onions, coarsely chopped
2 jalapeño peppers, finely chopped
¼ cup cider vinegar
3 tablespoons honey
1 teaspoon salt

1 Combine cabbage, tomatoes, green onions, jalapeños, vinegar, honey and salt in serving bowl; mix well. Cover and chill at least 2 hours before serving.

2 Stir well immediately before serving.

Makes 4 servings

Nutrients per Serving:

Calories	98
(4% of calories from fat)	
Total Fat	<1 g
Saturated Fat	<1 g
Cholesterol	0 mg
Sodium	564 mg
Carbohydrate	25 g
Dietary Fiber	3 g
Protein	2 g
Calcium	77 mg
Iron	1 mg
Vitamin A	96 RE
Vitamin C	90 mg

DIETARY EXCHANGES:
4 Vegetable

❖

Cook's Tip
For a milder cole slaw, discard the seeds and veins when chopping the jalapeños, as this is where much of the heat of the peppers is stored.

❖

INDIAN-STYLE VEGETABLE STIR-FRY

Using canola oil is an easy way to reduce the amount of saturated fat in stir-fries. Canola oil is rapidly becoming more popular in the U.S., as health-conscious cooks learn it contains more monounsaturated fat (the "better" fat) than any oil except olive oil. It even contains omega-3 fatty acids, which have been found to lower cholesterol and triglycerides. Canola oil is mild in flavor, so it can be used in salad dressings as well as cooking.

1 teaspoon canola oil
1 teaspoon curry powder
1 teaspoon ground cumin
⅛ teaspoon red pepper flakes
1½ teaspoons finely chopped, seeded jalapeño pepper
2 cloves garlic, minced
¾ cup chopped red bell pepper
¾ cup thinly sliced carrots
3 cups cauliflower florets
½ cup water, divided
½ teaspoon salt
2 teaspoons finely chopped cilantro (optional)

1 Heat oil in large nonstick skillet over medium-high heat. Add curry powder, cumin and red pepper flakes; cook and stir about 30 seconds.

2 Stir in jalapeño and garlic. Add bell pepper and carrots; mix well to coat with spices. Add cauliflower; reduce heat to medium.

3 Stir in ¼ cup water; cook and stir until water evaporates. Add remaining ¼ cup water; cover and cook about 8 to 10 minutes or until vegetables are crisp-tender, stirring occasionally.

4 Add salt; mix well. Sprinkle with cilantro and garnish with mizuna and additional red bell pepper, if desired. Serve immediately.

Makes 6 servings

Nutrients per Serving:

Calories	40
(22% of calories from fat)	
Total Fat	1 g
Saturated Fat	<1 g
Cholesterol	0 mg
Sodium	198 mg
Carbohydrate	7 g
Dietary Fiber	1 g
Protein	2 g
Calcium	27 mg
Iron	1 mg
Vitamin A	569 RE
Vitamin C	90 mg

DIETARY EXCHANGES:
1½ Vegetable

SPICY CORN MUFFINS

Who can resist fresh, warm corn muffins just out of the oven? Buttermilk gives a lighter texture to these muffins, so the sassy flavors of chili pepper and spices can't be missed. Try other flavorings for a change of pace, such as chopped onion, carrot, bell pepper or a pinch of chili powder.

1 cup low fat buttermilk
1 tablespoon vegetable oil
1 egg white
1 serrano pepper, minced
1 cup cornmeal
⅓ cup all-purpose flour
1 tablespoon finely chopped fresh cilantro or parsley
1 teaspoon baking powder
½ teaspoon baking soda
¼ teaspoon salt
¼ teaspoon ground cumin
¼ teaspoon ground paprika

1 Preheat oven to 400°F. Spray 6-cup muffin pan with nonstick cooking spray.

2 Combine buttermilk, oil, egg white and serrano pepper in small bowl until smooth.

3 Combine cornmeal, flour, cilantro, baking powder, baking soda, salt, cumin and paprika in medium bowl; mix well. Make a well in dry ingredients; pour in buttermilk mixture. Stir with fork just until dry ingredients are moistened.

4 Spoon batter evenly into muffin cups. Bake 15 to 20 minutes or until toothpick inserted in center comes out clean.

Makes 6 muffins

Nutrients per Serving:

Calories	140
(22% of calories from fat)	
Total Fat	3 g
Saturated Fat	1 g
Cholesterol	2 mg
Sodium	308 mg
Carbohydrate	23 g
Dietary Fiber	3 g
Protein	4 g
Calcium	62 mg
Iron	1 mg
Vitamin A	22 RE
Vitamin C	4 mg

DIETARY EXCHANGES:
1½ Starch/Bread, ½ Fat

❖

Cook's Tip
If you don't have buttermilk on hand, substitute 1 tablespoon vinegar or lemon juice plus enough milk to equal 1 cup. Stir and let stand 5 minutes before using.

❖

CONFETTI BLACK BEANS

❖

Originally from South America, black beans are also called turtle beans or frijoles negros, *their Spanish name. Black beans are a near-perfect food. They are low in fat, calories and sodium and are also cholesterol free. Just serve over rice to form a complete protein food source.*

❖

1 cup dried black beans
3 cups water
1 can (14 ounces) ⅓-less-salt chicken broth
1 bay leaf
1½ teaspoons olive oil
1 medium onion, chopped
¼ cup chopped red bell pepper
¼ cup chopped yellow bell pepper
2 cloves garlic, minced
1 jalapeño pepper, finely chopped
1 large tomato, seeded and chopped
½ teaspoon salt
⅛ teaspoon black pepper
   Hot pepper sauce (optional)

1 Sort and rinse black beans. Cover with water and soak overnight; drain. Place beans in large saucepan with chicken broth; bring to a boil over high heat. Add bay leaf. Reduce heat to low; cover and simmer about 1½ hours or until beans are tender.

2 Heat oil in large skillet over medium heat. Add onion, bell peppers, garlic and jalapeño; cook 8 to 10 minutes or until onion is tender, stirring frequently. Add tomato, salt and black pepper; cook 5 minutes.

3 Add onion mixture to beans; cook 15 to 20 minutes. Remove bay leaf before serving. Serve with hot sauce and garnish, if desired.

Makes 6 servings

Nutrients per Serving:

Calories	132
(12% of calories from fat)	
Total Fat	2 g
Saturated Fat	<1 g
Cholesterol	0 mg
Sodium	191 mg
Carbohydrate	23 g
Dietary Fiber	4 g
Protein	8 g
Calcium	34 mg
Iron	2 mg
Vitamin A	60 RE
Vitamin C	39 mg

DIETARY EXCHANGES:
1½ Starch/Bread,
½ Vegetable

*Personalized Nutrition Reference for Different Calorie Levels**

Daily Calorie Level	1,600	2,000	2,200	2,800
Total Fat	53 g	65 g	73 g	93 g
% of Calories from Fat	30%	30%	30%	30%
Saturated Fat	18 g	20 g	24 g	31 g
Carbohydrate	240 g	300 g	330 g	420 g
Protein	46 g**	50 g	55 g	70 g
Dietary Fiber	20 g***	25 g	25 g	32 g
Cholesterol	300 mg	300 mg	300 mg	300 mg
Sodium	2,400 mg	2,400 mg	2,400 mg	2,400 mg
Calcium	1,000 mg	1,000 mg	1,000 mg	1,000 mg
Iron	18 mg	18 mg	18 mg	18 mg
Vitamin A	1,000 RE	1,000 RE	1,000 RE	1,000 RE
Vitamin C	60 mg	60 mg	60 mg	60 mg

* Numbers may be rounded
** 46 g is the minimum amount of protein recommended for all calorie levels below 1,800.
*** 20 g is the minimum amount of fiber recommended for all calorie levels below 2,000.

Note: These calorie levels may not apply to children or adolescents, who have varying calorie requirements. For specific advice concerning calorie levels, please consult a registered dietitian, qualified health professional or pediatrician.

VOLUME MEASUREMENTS (dry)

⅛ teaspoon = 0.5 mL
¼ teaspoon = 1 mL
½ teaspoon = 2 mL
¾ teaspoon = 4 mL
1 teaspoon = 5 mL
1 tablespoon = 15 mL
2 tablespoons = 30 mL
¼ cup = 60 mL
⅓ cup = 75 mL
½ cup = 125 mL
⅔ cup = 150 mL
¾ cup = 175 mL
1 cup = 250 mL
2 cups = 1 pint = 500 mL
3 cups = 750 mL
4 cups = 1 quart = 1 L

VOLUME MEASUREMENTS (fluid)

1 fluid ounce (2 tablespoons) = 30 mL
4 fluid ounces (½ cup) = 125 mL
8 fluid ounces (1 cup) = 250 mL
12 fluid ounces (1½ cups) = 375 mL
16 fluid ounces (2 cups) = 500 mL

WEIGHTS (mass)

½ ounce = 15 g
1 ounce = 30 g
3 ounces = 90 g
4 ounces = 120 g
8 ounces = 225 g
10 ounces = 285 g
12 ounces = 360 g
16 ounces = 1 pound = 450 g

DIMENSIONS

1/16 inch = 2 mm
⅛ inch = 3 mm
¼ inch = 6 mm
½ inch = 1.5 cm
¾ inch = 2 cm
1 inch = 2.5 cm

OVEN TEMPERATURES

250°F = 120°C
275°F = 140°C
300°F = 150°C
325°F = 160°C
350°F = 180°C
375°F = 190°C
400°F = 200°C
425°F = 220°C
450°F = 230°C

BAKING PAN SIZES

Utensil	Size in Inches/Quarts	Metric Volume	Size in Centimeters
Baking or	8×8×2	2 L	20×20×5
Cake Pan	9×9×2	2.5 L	22×22×5
(square or	12×8×2	3 L	30×20×5
rectangular)	13×9×2	3.5 L	33×23×5
Loaf Pan	8×4×3	1.5 L	20×10×7
	9×5×3	2 L	23×13×7
Round Layer	8×1½	1.2 L	20×4
Cake Pan	9×1½	1.5 L	23×4
Pie Plate	8×1¼	750 mL	20×3
	9×1¼	1 L	23×3
Baking Dish	1 quart	1 L	—
or Casserole	1½ quart	1.5 L	—
	2 quart	2 L	—